NEW YEAR EDITION! – HIGH QUALITY ONLY FOR SERIOUS READERS

Tested & Found Working Perfectly In 2017

Easy **$500 A Day**
Without having any website or a product!
(Using Clickbank)

<u>Disclaimer</u>

The information presented herein represents the views of the author as of the date of publication. Because of the rate with which conditions change, the author reserves the rights to alter and update his opinions based on the new conditions. This manual is for informational purposes only and the author does not accept any responsibilities for any liabilities resulting from the use of this information. While every attempt has been made to verify the information provided here, the author and his referrals cannot assume any responsibility for errors, inaccuracies or omissions. Any slights of people or organizations are unintentional.

This publication is not intended for use as any source of advice such as legal, medical, or accounting. The publisher wants to stress that the information contained herein may be subject to varying international, federal, state, and/or local laws or regulations. The purchaser or reader of this publication assumes responsibility for the use of these materials and information. Adherence to all applicable laws and regulations, including international, federal, state and local governing professional licensing, business practices, advertising, and all other aspects of doing business in the EU, US, Canada or any other jurisdiction is the sole responsibility of the purchaser or reader. Neither the author nor the publisher assume any responsibility or liability whatsoever on the behalf of the purchaser or reader of these materials. Any perceived slight of any individual or organization is purely unintentional.

This book is for personal use only. It should serve as a reference only with no guarantee to any personal or financial gains. Results from usage of materials described in this book may vary. By reading this material, you agree that the author is not liable on any consequences arising from usage of this book.

Important Information From The Author

Dear reader, I am using this method of making money from last 2 years and it is working great for me. There is **not even a single day** when I did not make money through this method. To give true value to my readers, I keep checking the working of this method regularly on new Facebook accounts on regular intervals. To make sure whether this method is working correctly or not, I checked the authenticity of this method today itself (i.e. on 07th Jan 2017), I followed this method in a step by step manner and I found it working perfectly & flawlessly. I applied it on a totally new Facebook account which I made today itself, in the morning. I added friends by using the strategy mentioned in this PDF and within 6 hours I was making money. I took latest screenshots of my Facebook account, Clickbank account and income proofs today (i.e. on 07th Jan 2017) and inserted them in this PDF to give you the latest perspective and analysis.

One more thing that I want to add is that Facebook makes only minor changes in the interface of its website after every few months, so you should not worry about the changes that Facebook makes. You should apply this method without any hesitation and if you follow it in step by step manner, then I am sure that you will start making $60-$100 a day in just 3 days and you will be making $500 a day within just 4 weeks and it is my personal guarantee

vinay roy

This page intensionally left blanck

WELCOME TO HOW TO EARN MASSIVE AMOUNT USING FACEBOOK

Know Your Rights!

You have got one of the very few copies available free of cost on my website while other users had to pay **$97.00** to secure a copy of this method but I want to give you the same rights which are available to the paid customers. To give you the full value of your time and money I am offering you the following rights on this PDF report. You can do the following with this PDF.

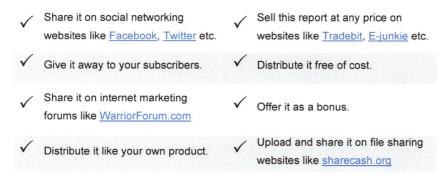

✓ Share it on social networking websites like Facebook, Twitter etc.

✓ Sell this report at any price on websites like Tradebit, E-junkie etc.

✓ Give it away to your subscribers.

✓ Distribute it free of cost.

✓ Share it on internet marketing forums like WarriorForum.com

✓ Offer it as a bonus.

✓ Distribute it like your own product.

✓ Upload and share it on file sharing websites like sharecash.org

Please Note, You Do <u>NOT</u> Have Any Right To Edit This Report.

Something About Me!

Hello friends, my name is vinay roy and I am a reputed member on many internet marketing forums & websites. Today, thousands of people from United Kingdom, USA, Canada, Australia, South Africa, UAE, Switzerland, Norway, India, Nigeria & Sri Lanka and many other countries know me for publishing the most realistic internet marketing e-books & reports. Every week, a lot of new people on the internet become my students, learn internet marketing from me and start making money successfully. I never hurry while publishing an e-book. I do research, find new methods & apply them and if I am successful, I tell others about those methods in my e-books. I write an e-book once in 6 months, but it is always the best one. For your information, I will keep publishing newer versions of 'Facebook Wealth Formula' and you can get them delivered to your inbox automatically, if you subscribe to my newsletter. If you have any doubts regarding this method or you face any difficulty in implementing this method please email me at vinaykumar15091997@gmail.com

The amount i.e. $97.00 which you have invested in 'Facebook Wealth Formula' is going to be your best investment in your internet marketing business. I am sure that you will learn awesome stuff out of this e-book. If you are reading this e-book online then I suggest you to **download the e-book on your computer** from here and then start reading it. Reading online will not give you better understanding and hyperlinks in the e-book will not work too. So, it is better to download before you start reading.

If you want to know how many people are making money using Facebook Wealth Formula, how they rate this method and what is their satisfaction level, then please visit this page If you want to ask a question regarding

this method simply email me at _____

Ok, Guys! As you have got latest version of Facebook Wealth Formula and you might have checked the authenticity of this method too, so we must start now. You might have read so many e-books on making money online, but no e-book gives you any guarantee that you will make money, right? But, here is the most realistic and practical e-book you have ever read in your life. It is a complete blueprint of making rock solid income consistently! This is the exact method which I use to make **$500 a day** from my own Facebook account! By following this strategy, like hundreds of other users, you can also reach at **$500 a day in just 4 weeks**, starting from scratch!

Step 1: Visit www.facebook.com and create a new Facebook account. If you already have a Facebook account, do NOT use it because it has your personal friends and it is not going to make you any money. Your new Facebook account should look like a profile of 18-20 years old girl. Girls get more attention and gain friends quickly. Name should be sweet & common one. It shouldn't look like a fake profile. It should be sober, natural and simple. Go to www.images.google.com and find the pictures that represent girls like flowers, candles, lips, cleavage (*sorry girls*) etc. and upload one of them as your profile picture. Do not upload picture of someone other. Enter as much information as you can into your profile because people do not like empty profiles. *Simple eh!*

Step 2: After creating your new Facebook Account, it is the time to add friends to it. You can add maximum 5000 friends to your Facebook account. Your motive should be to exploit this opportunity as quickly as you can. This is the most important task. How much money you will make depends upon the number of friends you have. I will show you how I added **5000 friends in 7 days only** but you can start making money as soon as you have only 1000 friends (Just 2 days task).

Step 3: If you start adding friends manually, you can not add 1000 friends even in a year so we will use a strategy to add friends really fast! As per this strategy, you need to find a good email list generator. Please note, we are talking about an email list generator and NOT about an email extractor or email scraper or email harvester. NEVER use an email extractor, harvester or scraper because you are going to waste your time because an email extractor will simply harvest email addresses from the internet and give you the list of collected email addresses. There are so many problems in using an email extractor, harvester or scraper. First, an email extractor extracts & collects email addresses from the websites randomly so the number of email addresses is limited upto the email addresses available on the websites i.e just 100, 500 or 1000 email addresses. Second, it will also collect email addresses from the websites of business firms, companies, lawyers and doctors etc. which are of NO USE to you. Definitely, you would not like to send a friend request to a doctor, lawyer, advocate, carpenter or an accounting firm. It can put you in a serious problem. So, do not even think about collecting email addresses from the internet and using them to send friend requests. *Makes sense?*

An *email lists generator* is different from an email extractor/harvester/scraper and is more powerful than that. An *email lists generator* generates lists of supposed email addresses using common names of the people of the countries you want to target. These email addresses belong to the general public and not to the companies, firms or business houses. The best thing is that you can use different combinations of the names, keywords, domain names and random numbers to generate the lists of *millions of unique email addresses* by repeating the task. Using an *email lists generator* you can target any market in any country you want. For example, you can generate lists of email addresses of those people who are interested in making money, losing weight, poker, credit cards, music, websites, SEO, Twitter or Facebook applications etc. Not only this, you can also target any country you want e.g. UK, USA, UK, Canada, Spain, Nigeria, Australia and any other country. I downloaded and tested different email lists generators, one after another. It took me 2 weeks and I wasted around $1325 to find the right tool. Yes, after wasting $1325 and testing different softwares, I found 'Acute Email IDs Production Engine'. I found this tool very impressive because there are two main reasons behind that. **First,** it is the cheapest one in price amongst all the tools I tested and rejected. **Second,** it is user friendly, easy to use & very effective. The best feature is that it saves email addresses lists in the text file format (.txt) which is a very important requirement for our method. It is really cheap in price and you can easily afford it.

I know that I am taking risk by openly recommending a product. You might think that I want to sell you this software, right? **No!** This is not a crappy e-book which contains affiliate links from Clickbank or Commission Junction websites to make sales and earn commission. I am already making **$500 a day**, so few more dollars from affiliate commission would not change my life. I am recommending this software because I have already tried many other softwares after wasting a lot of time and money and I do not want you to *waste your time and money* like I did in searching for the right tool. Although, I have made a recommendation but you are still free to use any tool of your choice but if you are going to buy any software other than *Acute Email IDs Production Engine*, then please make sure it has following features:

- option to generate unlimited email addresses lists
- target any country you want
- target any niche you want
- add random numbers while generating emails
- save email lists in text file (.txt)
- view and remove email lists
- add names into the database
- add countries into the database.

To give you a clear idea, so that you do not get confused, I have designed a small image just for your understanding.

** **Note**: You have saved a lot of time and money by just viewing at this image because I have already done the research for you.**

While using email list generator from www.sagawebs.com I found that more than 80% of generated email addresses really existed and that was a very good thing. Means, if you generate a list of 4000 email addresses then 3200 will be real ones and this is a fantastic figure. You do not need to send emails to these people. Facebook has a special feature to invite these people.

Warning!

I have noticed that few websites are cheating the customers by promising that they will give you Acute Email IDs Production Engine at a less price but it is a fraud. Either they will take your money and will not give you anything or they will give you another software which will be of no use to you. Even if they give you Acute Email ID software, they would not be able to give you license key because the activation is online. You will have to buy Acute Email IDs Production Engine thereafter again and it will cost you even more money. So just avoid these websites as there is no need to take risk. I bought my email list generator i.e. Acute Email IDs Production Engine from www.sagawebs.com who is the **genuine** and **original seller** of this software. So, do not give your money to any scammer or any other website, simply visit www.sagawebs.com to get Acute Email IDs Production Engine which is the best email list generator that works perfectly.

Step 4: Using your email lists generator, generate an email addresses list and save it in a text file. It should not take more than 60 seconds. Acute Email IDs Production Engine automatically saves email addresses in the text files (.txt). If you are going to choose a different email lists generator then make sure that it has this feature because it is very important. Now, we can use this email list to invite people on Facebook but Facebook does not allow uploading an email list directly on its platform.

Step 5: We must upload this email list on Yahoo Mail website in order to invite people on Facebook using Yahoo Mail. The email list must be in special format to upload on Yahoo mail. I have uploaded this format for your convenience on my website. Click here to download 'contacts.csv' file on your computer which is already in that format which Yahoo Mail accepts. After downloading this file, open it in MS_Excel.

In case you do not have MS_Excel then you can install "OpenOffice" on your computer by downloading it from here, it is free! If you are using "OpenOffice", then right click on 'contacts.csv' file icon and choose Open With > OpenOffice.org Calc as shown in the image below:

On next window, it will ask how you would like to open this file. Make the following settings. Please note that the option 'Comma' should be checked and the option 'Space' should be unchecked. After doing these settings, click OK and file will open.

After opening, this file will look like as below. This is an empty file, because it is just a format which Facebook accepts.

Step 6: Now, open your **Text File** in which email addresses list (you just generated) was saved. Copy all email addresses from it, come back to 'contacts.csv' file, right click and paste all email addresses under the column '**E-mail Addresses**' as shown in the picture below. Leave all other columns blank.

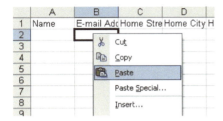

After pasting email addresses, 'contacts.csv' file will look like as below:

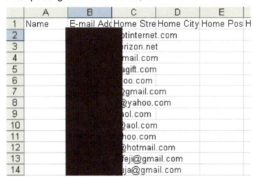

Step 7: When you save this file, MS_Excel (or OpenOffice) will ask you a new file name but you can simply overwrite the file choosing the same name. Choose 'Yes' if you see the following screen:

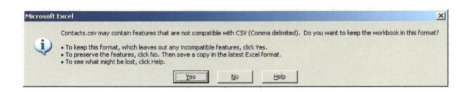

Trust me, you have done 60% work and are very close to **$500 a day**. Was it difficult? I do not think so! If you think it was difficult, then simply read it again and apply these steps while you are reading. You may find this process a bit boring, but remember **$500 a day** is not a small amount.

Here's the recap of all the steps performed till now:

1. Create a new Facebook account. Your profile should look like a profile of 18-20 years old girl. It should look simple, sober, natural and real.

2. Generate an email list using an email list generator of your choice. I used Acute Email IDs Production Engine. Do NOT use any email extractor, harvester or a scraper. You can instantly order it on www.sagawebs.com. Always beware from the scammers so go straight to www.sagawebs.com to buy genuine copy.

3. Download and install "OpenOffice" from here. (No need if you already have MS_Excel).

4. Download 'contacts.csv' file from this link: http://www.fbwealthformula.com/dl/docs.php I am offering this precious format, free of cost. Copy email addresses from text file and paste them in 'contacts.csv' file and save it.

Is it clear? Let's go further…

Step 8: Now, create a Yahoo mail account by visiting at mail.yahoo.com or any other link Yahoo offers. Creating Yahoo mail is a **60 seconds task**. After creating your account, login to Yahoo mail and click on 'contacts' icon as shown in the image below:

Step 9: Click 'Import Contacts' option on the next page.

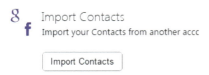

Step 10: Choose 'File upload' option on the next screen and click 'Import'.

File Upload
Upload a Contact file from y...

Import

Step 11: You will see the next window. Upload 'contacts.csv' file containing email addresses. Your email list will be imported into Yahoo mail account.

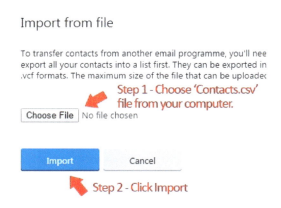

Import from file

To transfer contacts from another email programme, you'll nee export all your contacts into a list first. They can be exported in .vcf formats. The maximum size of the file that can be uploaded

Step 1 - Choose 'Contacts.csv' file from your computer.

Choose File | No file chosen

Import   Cancel

Step 2 - Click Import

Step 12: After successful import, it will show you the total contacts in your Yahoo mail.

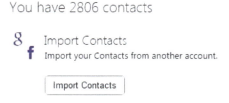

You have 2806 contacts

8 **f** Import Contacts
Import your Contacts from another account.

Import Contacts

Step 13: Now login to your Facebook account and then visit this link:

https://www.facebook.com/find-friends/browser/

      At this page, Facebook gives option to find your friends **by adding personal contacts**. You will see a lot of options to **add personal contacts** on this page. Yahoo mail is also one of them. Click on 'Yahoo Mail' icon. If Yahoo Mail is not available then click 'Other Email' icon.

Now, enter your Yahoo email and password on next window and your entire Yahoo contacts will be imported into new Facebook account.

Step 14: Now, Facebook will show you the list of contacts, it found in Yahoo Mail. Click 'Select All' checkbox and click 'Add to invite' button.

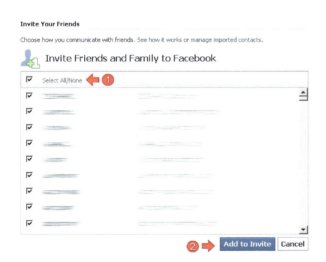

Step 15: You will see that Facebook has added all the friends in the invitation list. Now click 'Invite Your Friends' button and that's it! Facebook will send invitation to all these people. If the people on invitation list are already on Facebook then they will get friend request on your behalf and if they are not on Facebook, then they will get an invitation to join Facebook to become your friends.

Step 16: After sending invitations, open 'contacts.csv' file again and delete all email addresses from it. To invite more people, simply generate a fresh list of email addresses using 'Acute Email IDs Production Engine' and paste it in 'contacts.csv' file and save the file again. Now, upload this file again on Yahoo and import into Facebook by repeating the same process. You can do it as many times as you want by generating fresh email addresses every time.

On first day, I sent **invitations to 800 people** and it took **just 20 minutes!**

Didn't you find it easy?

Yes! It is a very easy process. Apply this process while reading this e-book, it will make things a lot easier. Follow this practice only two times a day. It takes only 2 minutes to generate hundreds of email addresses.

Attention!

Like I said earlier, consider yourself **very lucky** that you have got your hands on this method while others are still struggling to make money. Not only this, the chances of your success are **high enough** because most of the people are lazy and they will not act on this report or they think that this method will not work for them. By the way, I can not find any logic behind such thinking. May be they are too pessimistic or so unlucky to be successful. Anyhow, it is good for you because when only few people will act on this report, your chances to **WIN** will be more because of low competition.

Ok, when I sent invitation to 800 friends on first day, 334 people were already on Facebook and they got friend requests immediately and the remaining 466 people who were not on Facebook got invitation to join Facebook via email.

…Result?

I added **26 friends in 1 hour** only.

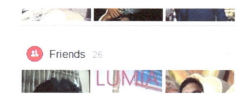

You know, Facebook activities go viral. When you add a friend, it is displayed on walls of both of you and a lot of other people notice your profile and because you have a girl profile, they also want to add you as a friend. Your work is just to accept these invitations.

See, how many friend requests I got <u>within next 2 hours</u>.

Yes, there were **39 friend requests** and my job was just to add them one by one.

Here is the screenshot of huge number of friend requests that I got on the same day I sent the invitations. As soon as you get friend requests, you can add them as your friends by clicking 'Confirm' button. I have blurred the names of Facebook users to protect their privacy, as per Facebook "Terms of use".

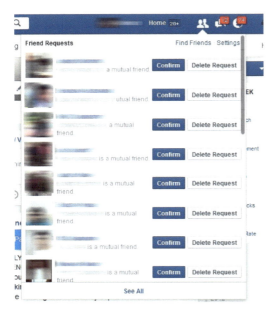

I added all of them as friends and now I had <u>63 friends</u> in just 3 hours.

After around **8 hours**, I checked again and got amazed that I had **more than 250 friends** in my Facebook account. **That was a fantastic figure!** Most of the people to whom I sent friend requests had added me (just because of 'hot' girl profile.) Means, I got more than **250 Facebook friends in just one day**! That was more than enough for me.

On **2ⁿᵈ Day**, I generated more email addresses using 'Acute Email IDs Production Engine' pasted them in 'contacts.csv' file and uploaded it on Yahoo Mail and then from Facebook invited more people choosing 'Yahoo Mail' as an option. This time I invited around 3000 people. Again, those who were already on Facebook got friend requests on my behalf and those who were not on Facebook got invitations via email. At an average, generating email lists and uploading 'contacts.csv' file was taking only few minutes. I was doing this process just 2 times a day so I was spending only <u>20-25 minutes</u> daily for this work.

On late evening of **2ⁿᵈ Day**, I checked my profile and found that I had **more than 600 friends.**

I was taking screenshots every day, because, I was an active member at <u>Digitalpoint Forum</u> and was sharing my progress in <u>this thread</u>. The forum members were so excited with the results that they started sharing their Facebook accounts urls and their personal email addresses to add even more friends, faster. It was against Facebook as well as Digitalpoint rules so forum moderators had to delete the thread.

Anyhow, now I was getting <u>70-90 friend requests daily</u> and was adding a lot of friends every day. I was uploading 'contacts.csv' file daily to my Yahoo Mail account and was using Facebook to invite contacts in my Yahoo Mail. I was using a fresh email list everyday as there is no limit on the number of email lists that you can generate using *Acute Email IDs Production Engine.*

I took this screenshot on **3rd Day**. Look at the huge jump in the number of friends.

Day – 3

Actually, Facebook does not allow you to send 20 or more friend requests manually but, when you invite them through this method, this limit does not apply.

On **5th Day**, I had more than **2200 friends**.

Now, I was getting thousands of likes for whatever I was sharing. Just have a look at this screenshot.

These "Likes" are for some images that I shared on my profile page, I had not created any Facebook page yet. You can share any item in which everyone is interested like images of Apple iPhone, Beautiful Cars, Romantic Quotes etc. etc.

See another picture of immense amount of "Likes"

👍 Like   💬 Comment   ➡ Share

😊❤️😲 You, Prince Tan and 1746 others

Day-6 - Ultimate Growth Day!

Hurray! This was the 7th **Day** & I achieved the target of adding **5000 friends**.

As you saw on the previous page, that I reached at 5000 friends in just 7 days but still, there were <u>a lot of pending friend requests</u> and when I tried to confirm them I got this message.

Like I already mentioned that maximum number of friends which you can add is 5000 but **you do not need to add 5000 friends and you can start making money <u>as soon as you have 1000 friends</u>**. So after I reached this number of friends, people could not send me friend requests anymore. If someone would send me a friend request he will see the following error message:

When you have 4000-5000 friends, you get immense exposure to anything you post. Look, I got 695 likes in **just 20 minutes** to a simple message I posted on my FB profile.

See, how many friends in my profile have birthday on same day, because I had a large number of friends, so there were a lot of birthdays on same day.

Once you reach at this level, your **<u>80% work</u>** is complete! I added 5000 friends in just 7 days, but you need only 1000 friends to make money so it can be completed only in 2 days ;)

Here is a quick summary of adding 5000 friends in 7 days only!

1. Visit www.facebook.com and create a new Facebook account.
2. Get a good email list generator. I use *Acute Email IDs Production Engine* from www.sagawebs.com but in case you are using another email lists generator then make sure it has the option to generate unlimited email lists and saving them in text files.
3. Visit this link: http://www.fbwealthformula.com/dl/docs.php and download a readymade file format to upload on Yahoo Mail, the name of the file is 'contacts.csv'. Yahoo Mail would not accept any format other than this one.
4. Open 'contacts.csv' in MS_Excel. If you do not have MS_Excel then you can download open office and install it on your computer. Thereafter, right click on 'contacts.csv' file icon and choose *open with > openoffice.org calc*
5. Copy email addresses from text file saved by Acute Email IDs Production Engine and paste them into 'contacts.csv' under the heading 'E-mail Addresses'. Leave other columns blank and save it.
6. Create a new Yahoo Mail account and upload *'contacts.csv'* file on your Yahoo mail account. It will import all email addresses from *contacts.csv*.
7. Thereafter click on this link: https://www.facebook.com/find-friends/browser/ and choose 'Yahoo Mail' as an option to import your contacts into Facebook to find friends.
8. After import, Facebook will show all the contacts.
9. Click 'Select All' and then click 'Add to Invite' button and then click 'Invite your friends'.
10. Do this process twice a day and you will get 5000 friends in just 7 days.

Summary of steps for generating email lists from Acute Email IDs Production Engine and importing into your Facebook account.

Acute Email IDs Production Engine   **Contacts.csv File**   **Yahoo Mail**   **Facebook**

Best Advice That You Can Ever Get!

As you have seen that it is too easy to add 5000 friends to your FB Account with the help of Acute Email IDs Production Engine, Contacts.csv file and Yahoo Mail. Still, if you think that it is difficult, then you should start doing this wonderful activity while reading this ebook. That means, starting & completing the tasks while reading the ebook. Go for step 1 and once it is completed, read and complete step 2 and so on. In that way, the time you will finish reading this ebook, you might have added significant number of FB friends to your account.

Step 16: Creating a Facebook Page - <mark>No Investment Required!</mark>

In order to make money from your Facebook account you must have a Facebook page. As soon as you have **just 1000 friends**, you can create a Facebook page and start making money from the same day. That means, if you start today, you can start making money within 4 days. (Adding 1000 friends takes 3 days only and you can create a Facebook page and start making money from 4th day). Although, it will be $50 - $70/day in the beginning but within just 4 weeks you will reach at $500/day. But even $50/day in just 4 days is a BIG achievement! *Isn't it?*

Let's understand it this way

If you start on	You will have 1000 Facebook friends on	You can create Facebook page and start making atleast $50/day from
Monday	Wednesday	Thursday
Tuesday	Thursday	Friday
Wednesday	Friday	Saturday
Thursday	Saturday	Sunday
Friday	Sunday	Monday
Saturday	Monday	Tuesday
Sunday	Tuesday	Wednesday

You can create a Facebook page on anything you want. It may be about a particular subject you like for example a celebrity, computers, mobiles, laptops, games, dating sites, matrimonial, weight loss, health tips or anything. All you need is a Facebook account and if you have a Facebook account with 1000 friends (which is very easy with email list generator), **then *you have gold in your hands!***

After creating a Facebook page, you can start making money from the same day. You will start selling products and earning commissions from your fan page from **VERY FIRST DAY** and this is my promise. Not only this, as the number of 'Likes' for your fan page increases, you will get even more 'Likes' automatically at a rapid speed and you will make more money every day on complete autopilot!

Most Important Lesson - Remember

Before creating a fan page, you must have at least 1000 friends. That does not mean that you can not create a fan page without having 1000 friends but if you create a fan page before having 1000 friends, then your page will not get enough exposure and it will be difficult to earn money from it.

Let's move to the next step...

How To Create A Page That Brings Avalanche Of Money To You!

First of all, visit http://www.facebook.com/pages/create.php to start creating a page, choose "Cause or Community" as page type and fill in all the possible details into your fan page.

Local Business or Place

Company, Organization or Institution

Brand or Product

Artist, Band or Public Figure

Entertainment

Cause or Community

Add an attractive image to your page to gain more attention. If you want to create a picture yourself then you can visit Google Images to get an idea. If you find anything incomplete in your fan page then complete it first before asking your friends to join it. Besides it, your page should have an attractive and meaningful name which is related to the type of product you can easily sell.

For example, if you are interested in selling a product about "weight loss" then the title of your page can be any of the following:

- *Stay fit by losing a bit – Get free weight loss tips every day*
- *Lose weight quickly – free daily diet info*
- *Fast results – Ultimate weight loss tips*

After your page is complete in all respects, it is the time to make money :)

How to start making money without having any website or a product?

Because you do not have a website or a product to sell, so we will take help of Clickbank. Clickbank.com is a digital marketplace where thousands of products are sold every day. It is one of the most popular website for those people who want to make money online without any website or a product. It is completely free to join. Clickbank is that website where hundreds of informative products like ebooks, softwares and the membership sites are sold every day.

There're 3 types of people who use Clickbank:

1. **Vendors** – Those who create & sell the products like ebooks, softwares, memberships & courses on Clickbank. They are the sellers actually. Generally, the products sold on Clickbank are downloadable.
2. **Customers** - Those who buy the products from Clickbank website.
3. **Affiliates** – Those who spread the links of these Clickbank products on the internet to let people know about these products. When someone clicks on an affiliate link and buy the product, then affiliates earn commissions. Means, an affiliate is a middleman between customer and vendor (seller) and sends the customers to seller's website through his affiliate link to earn commission on every sale.

Note: You are going to work as an affiliate in this system.
Your work is just posting affiliate links of Clickbank products on your Facebook page and sending the customers to seller's website. You will earn commission as soon as someone buys something after clicking on your link.

Now, I will tell you how to make $500/day by working as Clickbank "affiliate" and using your Facebook page. You will get this money transferred to your bank account whenever you want. Your work is just posting the links of Clickbank products on Facebook. When someone clicks on your link and buy any product, you will earn commission. The commissions on the products are really high and ranges from **50% - 85%** of price of the product. That means, if you post a link to a $50 product and commission is 60% then **you will get $30 for just ONE SALE!**

You do not have to do anything as your work is just sending the customers to vendor's product website, that's it! As soon as a sale is done through your link, the commission will be credited to your account and you can withdraw it whenever you want. Clickbank pays commissions via bank cheque or direct bank transfer. You can choose the option in your account. But you can enter your bank account details in your Clickbank account only after you have earned $100 in commission.

Creating a Clickbank account: So just visit at www.clickbank.com and create a free account. Fill in all the required details in your account to complete it in all respects.

A Secret Tip

In case you do not find your country name in the signup form on Clickbank, then do not worry. For example, if you are from Nigeria then you will not find "Nigeria" as an option in the list of countries, but still you can create account on Clickbank and earn commissions. While signing up on Clickbank, enter any fake address and choose any country like USA. After you have earned $100 in your Clickbank account, you can enter your bank account details there and money will be transferred to your bank account and it does not matter in which country you are located. They will ask you just your Bank Name, Bank Account Number and Bank Branch Code (Mentioned on your bank cheque book) and you will start receiving money in your bank account **even if** you are in that country which is not in Clickbank's list. Now, please do not share this tip with anyone. ☺☺☺

Step 15: Generating your affiliate link:

After logging into your Clickbank account you can start making money instantly. Simply visit this link: https://accounts.clickbank.com/account/marketplace.htm This is the marketplace of the Clickbank where you can see all the products being sold on Clickbank. At this page, you will see an option to find the products:

Enter any keyword to find the products according to your taste. For example, if you can sell products related to "Weight Loss" then enter "weight loss" as your keyword and if your interest is in "Forex" then enter "Forex" to find the products. After entering the keyword, you will get a list of lot of products. There's a button saying "Promote" in front of each of the product like shown below. Click on the "Promote" button in front of that product which you choose to promote. You must **read this article** which tells how to choose the best products to promote. But do not make it so hard, just choose any product whose price, commissions and the website appeals you.

When you click "Promote", a popup window will appear. In the popup window, enter your Clickbank Nickname and click "Create" to generate the affiliate link of that product. **Nickname is generally the username of your Clickbank account** and is automatically entered while generating affiliate link.

In the next window the HopLink (affiliate link) will appear in the first field and HTML code in the second field. Copy the HopLink URL from the first field. You do **NOT** need the HTML code. That's it!

"Hoplink" or "affiliate link" is the same thing

Congratulations! Now you have your own affiliate link or hoplink. This hoplink has a Tracking ID linked to your Clickbank account. Now when a visitor clicks on your hoplink, he will be redirected to the website of that product which you selected to promote and if the visitor makes a purchase, you will earn commission.

Testing your hoplink (affiliate link): It is important to check your hoplink (or affiliate link), before you proceed further. To test, if your Hoplink (or affiliate link) is working accurately or not, paste the HopLink into internet browser (internet explorer, chrome, firefox etc.) address bar and hit Enter. The HopLink will take you to the product website. Read the sales page and, just for testing purpose, click something like "Purchase Now/Buy Now/Download Now" etc. on that page, just like you are a buyer. You will see the order form page. Scroll down to the bottom of the order page like shown in the image below.

1. If your affiliate link is working properly, you should see: [affiliate = yournickname]
2. If your affiliate link is not working properly, you will see: [affiliate = none]

Below shown picture shows a working affiliate link in which username of a Clicbank affiliate is showing up.

Now, you have your hoplink ready and we need people who click on your link and buy the product. Remember, the more clicks you get, the more sales will be there and more commissions you will earn. Never post any HopLink on your Facebook wall otherwise you will be blocked by Facebook and your account will be deleted. You can post Clickbank HopLinks only on a Facebook page created by you.

Now, lets start earning money with your first post

You already have a Facebook page, now it is the time to post "Status" and tell your friends about it. "Status" is a message that you want to share with your fans. I promote "Weight Loss" products. Every day, I post a free tip on losing weight + affiliate link (hoplink) as a "Status". I find new tips every day from the internet and post them on my page with my Clickbank affiliate link. Here's an example of an ideal "Status":

After posting a status update, click "Build Audience" button on your page and then click on "Invite Friends" option.

It will open a widget "Invite Friends" on your fan page. In that widget Facebook shows all of your 5000 friends and there is a button 'Invite' in front of the name of every friend.

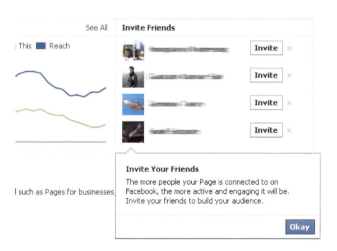

Once you click "Invite" button in front of your friend name, Facebook will send invitation to your friend to join your fan page. Unfortunately, Facebook does not allow inviting all the friends in one go. So, you can invite them only <u>one by one</u> and it makes it a time consuming task. But remember, once you have invited all of your friends, you will get a lot of clicks on your affiliate link and will earn a lot of commission in a really short period of time. If you can not finish inviting all the friends in one day or in one sitting then no problem! You can invite the remaining friends on another day and so on. Remember, the more friends you invite the more money you will be making so do not be lazy in inviting the friends. Once someone "Likes" your page, he starts getting updates about your fan page on his wall, automatically. Means, your fans will get notification every time you post something on your page.

How to make your fan page go viral!

<u>Tip 1</u>: Keep posting newer things on your wall about your fan page. Ask people to join your fan page to get free tips in your niche. Repeat this process few times a day and you will be amazed on seeing the tremendous growth.

<u>Tip 2</u>: Use 'Discussion' tab on your page to start discussions on your topic like 'weight loss' in my case. People like conversations and sharing ideas. Give them some tips and they will share their tips too. This is really simple, just like chatting on your Yahoo messenger or any other discussion forum. You will also have administrative rights of your fan page, so enjoy it!

May I Tell You Again?

Like I said earlier that you can start making money from 4th Day because in 2 days you can add 1000 friends. On 3rd Day, you can create a fan page and post something with your affiliate link and on 4th Day, you can invite your friends to your fan page. As they will read your post and like to know more, they will definitely click on your affiliate link and will buy something from the website you are promoting.

As soon as I had 1000 friends, I started inviting friends to my fan page. It took me 7 days to add 5000 friends but on the other hand, I was also inviting my FB friends to my page. I finished inviting 5000 friends in 10 days, but you can do this task in just 1 day, because you can start inviting them as soon as you have 1000 friends. When I finished inviting all of my 5000 friends on 10th day midnight, I went to the bed feeling tired and sleepy. When I checked my Facebook account on 11th day (next day) noon, I got a big surprise! I saw that **533 users** liked my fan page and it was a huge response.

When one of your friends "Like" your page, it is posted on his wall. Some of his friends may also like to visit your page and "Like" it and then their friends & so on… Your work is just to wait and watch now! So, when on first day, 533 users liked my fan page, it was posted on their walls and you can imagine how much exposure my fan page got on the same day.

Day - 12 - Next day, when I checked the stats, I almost jumped in the air! See the viral growth! It is RAPID!

Photos   Likes

Day-13 – More than 100% increase in "Likes".

Photos   Likes

Day-14 (A day of tremendous growth, this is how Facebook works in a viral way)

Photos   Likes

Day-17

Photos   Likes

Day-19

Photos   Likes

Day-22

Photos   Likes

Day-24

Photos   Likes

Day-26

Photos   Likes

Day – 28

Photos   Likes

On 29th Day, I had <u>more than 50000 Fans</u> – 2nd Target Achieved!!

Photos   Likes

<u>**Remember: You must have minimum 1000 friends to share your page**</u> otherwise, your page will not be popular. Your first target should be to add atleast 1000 friends to your FB account. This is totally easy and can be achieved in just 48 hours like I showed you. I showed you that 50,000 "Likes" can be gained in just 30 days but you do not need to get 50,000 "Likes" to make money because you will start making money even when you have **just 200 "Likes"**.

<u>Remember: As soon as you have 1000 FB friends and 200 'Likes' you will start making money.</u>

How many posts & how much effective they are?

Just 2-3 posts a day will be enough. It shouldn't take more than 25-30 minutes a day. I post health tips, weight loss tips, diet information with my Clickbank affiliate links as status updates. You should encourage your fans to click on your affiliate link to get more information about the products.

Let me show you the stats of my fan page that only administrator of the page can view.

Let me show you the screenshot of the dashboard, only the administrator can view it.

By viewing these images, you can get idea about the traffic that I am receiving and the number of clicks which I am getting on my affiliate links. The more "Likes" means more traffic and more traffic means more click and sales.

May I show you another screenshot of ultimate exposure that I am getting from my Facebook page. One day, I made a post about a unique product and you can see how many people viewed and liked my "Status" and how many people on Facebook shared it with others. That is totally INSANE! On that day **I got 1022 hits** on my affiliate link and made **$1148 on the same day!**

Lets Calculate Your Earning

Now suppose, you are too bad in writing posts and most of the people ignore your posts. But still if only 1% of your fans click on your affiliate link and make purchases (this is minimum), then you will get at least 2 sales a day, and this is just the beginning. With the passage of time, you will get more friends, more likes and more sales.

200 fans X 1% = 2 sales a day - This is just the beginning

What if you have 50,000 "Likes" like I have?

The figures I showed you are really easy to achieve and we've taken everything at its minimum. For example, getting 1000 FB friends is really easy with the help of a good email list generator like Acute Email IDs Production Engine. Once you have 1000 friends then having 200 "Likes" is too easy and just a childish game. Having 200 Likes means you can start making money because if only 1% people read and purchase the items from your affiliate links then you will start getting 2 sales a day.

Let me show you my Clickbank earnings!

WEEKLY SALES SNAPSHOT

Week Ending	Gross Sales
2017-01-10 (current week)	$3866.70
2017-01-03	$3850.08
2016-12-27	$4028.19
2016-12-20	$2612.66
2016-12-13	$3749.11

DAILY SALES SNAPSHOT

CLICKBANK INSIGHTS

ClickBank Insights provides you wi
your customers' buyer behavior. R
transactions across our entire netw

At this time your account has not re
display ClickBank insights.

Visit the Knowledge Base for more

Date		Gross	Trend
Sat	Jan 07	$524.53	
Fri	Jan 06	$554.20	
Thu	Jan 05	$600.36	
Wed	Jan 04	$517.42	
Tue	Jan 03	$521.96	
Mon	Jan 02	$584.74	
Sun	Jan 01	$563.49	
Sat	Dec 31	$520.06	
Fri	Dec 30	$536.76	
Thu	Dec 29	$605.90	
Wed	Dec 28	$503.29	
Tue	Dec 27	$526.66	
Mon	Dec 26	$600.58	
Sun	Dec 25	$556.83	
Sat	Dec 24	$565.22	

Best Thing About Clickbank!

The best thing about Clickbank is that it pays you through online bank transfer. If you do not have a bank account, then you can get a bank account by going to a nearby bank where you live. As soon as you earn $100 in your Clickbank account, you can enter your bank details and Clickbank will send your earnings to your bank account and thereafter whenever your earnings level reaches at $100 it will be transferred to your bank account, automatically!

I remain too busy in my other online businesses and internet marketing campaigns, so I do not get time to post 2-3 updates daily. I usually post only 3-4 posts in a week and I manage to get around 20 sales a day because I keep getting traffic from previous posts too. I usually promote products which give commission of $20-$30 per sale, so I make $500/day really easy. You will not believe to make $500/day I do not have to do ANYTHING except posting some updates on my fan page. **This is 100% autopilot!** I feel so safe about my family, life and the future because this is 100% secure and surefire way of making money from your Facebook account without any investment, website or a product. In the beginning, you will have easy 2-3 sales a day which will make you around $50-$60 a day but soon you will have more friends, more fans and more clicks on your affiliate links. You can reach $500/day in just 4 weeks, like I showed you. *Just imagine, how your life will change if you start making $500/day with just 30 minutes a day.*

Here are some of the other products which will sell easily on Facebook. Because majority of the Facebook users are 20-40 years old, so you can sell anything amongst the following:

- Weight Loss (Hot niche)
- Games, Music and MP3 (Hot niche)
- Acne Treatment (Hot niche)
- Dating offers (Hot niche)
- Pregnancy control
- Teen parenting
- Facebook applications
- Surveys etc.
- Mobile ringtones etc. (Hot niche)

A true short story

Few weeks back, my sister in law asked me to recommend her a good method to make money online and I gave her a copy of Facebook Wealth Formula. She applied it and added **1200** FB fans in just **4 days** and now she is simply offering Clickbank products to her Facebook friends & fans and guess what? She's making more than <u>**$150 a day**</u> in commissions and it is <u>without</u> any website and own product.

There are a lot of opportunities to make money with Facebook. Once you have got around 1000 friends, you can offer them surveys to complete, sell your own product, direct Facebook traffic to your website or blog, you can offer them "Email Submit" offers and much more and you can make a lot of cash with your FB friends. The main thing is adding friends to your account which can be easily done with an email list generator. There are a lot of websites who pay you for just sending visitors to their websites and having them fill a simple online form or just submitting their email addresses on the website. **Always remember,** once you have added 1000 friends then there is GOLD in your hands and you just need to monetize that traffic. Your top most task should be to add 1000 friends in your FB account and that can be done in just 2 days. Thereafter you can start making money really simple by just monetizing Facebook traffic.

Here Is The Guarantee Of Your Success
– You Would not Believe –

You would not believe but if you follow the below strategy then it is guaranteed that you will be successful! I do not want you to just read this e-book and close it. I want you to become successful in making money with your Facebook account, so, I am going to help you even further. If you are really determined about changing your life, then just email me at admin@highspeedbusiness.net with the subject:

I am ready to implement FWF

In the email body, you can write anything that you want to discuss.

Please note, before sending email, you must make sure that you have completed **two simple tasks** so that I can be sure that you are really determined about making money and not wasting my time.

Task 1: You must have created a new Facebook account and a Clickbank account. Your existing FB account will not work and it does not matter how many friends you have. So, you must have both of these accounts – a new FB account and a new Clickbank account.

Task 2: You must have bought Acute Email IDs Production Engine from www.sagaweb.com or any other good email list generator which works like Acute.

As soon as you complete these simple two tasks, send me an email immediately at vinaykumar15091997@gmail.com with subject line: **I am ready to implement FWF**

(There is no need to send any email if you do not have any question and you think that can implement this system yourself. **You are genius! Yes, you can do it at your own.***)*

Trust me, as soon as I get your email I will tell you about those Clickbank products which you can promote on your Facebook account and can earn $100 in just 48 hours – my personal guarantee!

Do Not Implement This Method Without Verifying

For the convenience of my readers, I check and implement this method on fresh Facebook accounts regularly and verify the working of this method on regular intervals. Before implementing this method, I suggest you to confirm whether this method is working or not . This _____

link will show you the date of last verification and will tell you whether this method can be implemented today or not.

_____

A lot of people after reading "Facebook Wealth Formula" are making **more than $100 a day** in their first week. Click here to see, how many people from UK, USA, Canada, Australia, Africa, Nigeria, India and Sri Lanka and many other countries are making money with Facebook Wealth Formula. I have spent a really long time to develop this perfect system which guarantees that you will be making $500 a day within 4 weeks. I do not want you to just read and close this e-book. My purpose is not to just 'sell' you this guide and earn $97.00. I want to make you successful in making money with this perfect system, so that you tell others too about this ebook. If you really want to make money, then just reading this report is not enough, you will have to 'take action'. Most of the people do not make any money because they just read, read & read but do not take any action. So, do yourself a favor, do not let this opportunity go, because this opportunity will not come back! Stop thinking and start doing.

TAKE ACTION NOW!
It is Time To Make Money
& Show The World What You Are!!!

Click here for a typical action plan

Have a great luck!
Your Friend

vinay roy

TYPICAL ACTION PLAN

Day 1

Start right now and download all the important and necessary items, right away.

A. Create your Facebook account and complete your profile accordingly as mentioned in this e-book earlier.

B. Buy Acute Email IDs Production Engine from www.sagawebs.com download it and get used to it. Check how email lists generator works and how to generate and save email lists on your computer.

C. Create your Clickbank account (no need if you already have a website and a product to sell). Understand Clickbank marketplace and how affiliate links work.

Day 2

Create necessary accounts:

D. Send me an email (vinaykumar15091997@gmail.com) with subject: **"I am ready to implement FWF"**. No need to send email if you can implement FWF yourself and you do not have any question. You can master it, trust me!

E. Download 'OpenOffice' and install it on your computer (No need if you already have MS_Excel).

F. Download 'contacts.csv' file from here

Day 3

After you have everything set and ready, start applying this method without any delay. Read all the steps of this e-book again and try to apply them while you are reading.

If you follow this method in the same manner as I have described then I am sure, you will start making money in just **4 days straight and it is my personal guarantee!** In case you have any doubt, contact me at vinaykumar15091997@gmail.com

vinay roy

www.ingramcontent.com/pod-product-compliance
Lightning Source LLC
Chambersburg PA
CBHW041146050326
40689CB00001B/513